Charlotte

Jamie Shaw

Executive Press Ltd
Edmonton AB T6A 0H7
Canada
343-554-1210

The views expressed in this work are solely those of the author and do not necessarily reflect the views of the publisher, and the publisher hereby disclaims any responsibility for them.

Paperback ISBN: 979-8-9913174-9-8
Ebook ISBN: 979-8-9987482-0-2

Charlotte

∞ ∞ ∞

Jamie Shaw

L'espoir, l'esprit, l'amour;
Tout je te donne, Chérie:
Je vois ton cœur en or
De loin, et je souris …

For He Who Hath Nothing
[one]

For he who hath nothing—
What? Sunshine wilt give?
In light for the loving,
A reason to live?

This cursing and cussing—
Abhorrent the sound
Dispersing their rushing,
Condemning thy mound ...

They spar with contentment,
As, caught in its beam,
Must harbour resentment
Sorority's dream

Ineffable, militant,
Worse for the wear,
As hornets fly, sibilant,
Combing the air,

Lest bishops and sailors,
Like tradies of dope,
Seek wisdom in tailors
With just enough rope.

On A Black Planet
[two]

Alone in a universe
Lost in its size:

Doth hope in a puny, terse
Eloquence rise
If, seething with tolerance,
Wrought within peace,
Devotion's our severance,
Love our release?

O Lover, thou knowest we
Fall to the floor
Of stuttering poetry
Comets adore,

When, on a black planet,
Consumptive with fire,
Two souls seek to fan it—
In callow desire!

Forgetting Not Ever Thee
[three]

Forgetting not ever thee, Giver of Love—
I couldn't, for thou art a smile within —
To fly like an Eagle, wilt thou be my Dove?
Lest ev'rything end, to let something be-
gin!

By lace so well hidden, yet written in space
Nigh features, impressions of loveliness
held
Thy face: Be my vixen, whom others will
chase—
My sutures internally irony's pelt

Eternally dwelling here deep in my heart's

Hues—sketches creational working to woo

The woman, the willfulness, woven by arts

Through which, given witchery, fog in the dew,

Mine Eden dost calibrate, sowing a plant

That wanting thee ent'reth, and willing thee can't.

Sun-Myrrh Sent
[four]

This morning, like a friend returns;
The night is over—come with me
Where daylight takes what sunshine burns
In pleasure, of her company ...

Oh, can't you hear the herons chirp,
The plovers warble—in the skies
Invernal clouds disperse: on Earth
Our day begins, as lovers rise

To greet the majesty of morn
In witness to my wonderment—
All over trials, tricks, and scorn,
As I with you, my Sun-Myrrh sent,

Lift eyes and hearts to days ahead,
In love your joys to peace have wed.

Stars in My Heart
[five]

I thought I was crazy, I dunno why—

When we were together, you see

I thought it was over: to bid love "Good-
Bye!"

Must Purgat'ry tolerate me ...

But love found a way—you're stars in my
heart,

Which, twinkling, are bursting with love:

For 'love' is a word from which I won't de-
part—

A wink in your Heavenly grove ...

I know I would die, to be left on a shore

Where bottles wash up, SOS

Your loveliness I thought just couldn't be more

Than blessings you bless me to bless—

So, you found a way: you are Love herself,

A box of sweet caramel goo

That's shining and sparkling high up on a shelf

Of "Thank-You's!" so partial to you!

Hearts
[six]

I love you, ev'rything about—
You say you love me more:
You're dear and comely, lean and stout,
Enough to just adore ...

You have your bunny, loving hearts
Can love so little else
Than love itself—like shopping carts
Now playing "Jingle Bells" ...

To think I thought we shouldn't win
The hearts that live and beat
Inside a cage where hope may sin
Impart, yet never meet.

Beyond Words
[seven]

The dearest hope you make come true,
The sweetest soul you are:
Of many women, less than few
Can lift my pen as far.

And yet—what's leaving ink upon
This page, cannot relate
The way the words are gone, in fond
Progression none can state

But you: Just hear the silence fall
In dew upon your tongue—
What rises isn't breath at all,
But you upon my lung!

Emma Forever
[eight]

O Light of my Life, must tarry without?

The light in our kitchen doth tarry within

The hopes for tomorrow I carry about

The joys which I'm hoping you'll carry within!

Lest loneliness linger, lost loving your wake,

Let loveliness lavish, in mem'ries behind,

Eternities: every giving or quake

Maternity's merit—to serve to remind

The Mother of Melodies, medicine's quill

May seemingly blanket, for she, in my heart,

Is succour for every reticent ill—

Till death come to take who will never depart.

Promised Land
[nine]

Wish I had the hots for Emma—
O My Goddess, what's that tremor
Pulsing like a soul dilemma
Through my tingling sticky-stemma?

Maybe she's my body's quest—
The one I'm on, the one I'm blest
To calibrate, corrall'd, caress'd,
Till deep inside her Perry's press'd!

I mustn't take her lightly, though
Her Lust-Gent hasn't far to go—
As crests and keyholes cape her nipples,
Honey dew, from top to tipples,

Ent'reth Promised Land's bedripples—
Brooks of bone, for lakes of lipples!

Rose of Loveliness
[ten]

O sweet Rose of Loveliness,
Sunlight's pin thou art—
Élite glow's up-above-liness
Caught within a heart

Where, budding, soon of blossoming,
Hopes together lope,
Ere, hearing moon or possum sing,
Slopes ought better cope

Through eyes, long lost in love-to-be,
Wistful as the dew
Requiting Eden's apple tree
Hungrily, for two.

Lorelei
[eleven]

Voluptress, wrap me up in chains,
I hear the sirens wail:
Seductress, in desire's reins
I am, for being male.

Just pamper me with lusty hopes,
Put balsam on my peace
You take away, as crusty soaps
Too batter'd for release.

Yes, lure me, once pure me,
To be a shipman spent
On vanity, a tour we
Began, but never meant.

For seven are the deadly sins—
I wasn't born to fry—
To get her balmy bed begins
Lament for Lorelei.

Twenty-One
[**twelve**]

I may be thirteen, eighteen even—
You are more than twelve:
Upon my teak you seek to weave
In coir spoors I delve.

The God of Love is hardly Fear—
Of You I am afraid:
His Goddess, close but never near
Is chastity, waylaid.

Oh, save me someone—You cannot,
Each day the rising Sun
Must, burning, ever rue his lot,
And quake for Twenty-One.

Tagestraum
[thirteen]

Ein Juwel, mehr als Schatz—Du bist
Der Brunnen tief in mir,
Wo ich ja weiter nichts denn Mist
Bin, wenn nicht tief in Dir.

Die Welt erwacht, da Du noch träumst
In Übersee, obschon
Das Herz, das bindet, Du versäumst
Daheim, in Trieb und Ton.

Ein Hund, entfernt, so eifrig bellt,
Als wäre er noch kaum
Am Leben, sondern in der Welt
Voll Lust auf Tagestraum.

Rêverie
[fourteen]

Emma, femme si bonne, si belle,
Surtout, pour son mari:
Si d'autres femmes le sont—laquelle
Qu'habite son cœur ravi

Est surpuissante, l'équivalence
De l'air dans ses poumons
En plein surcroît, la jolie dance
Des Papillons où vont

Sororité, fraternité
À partir de sa bouche
En liberté, égalité,
Qu'en verité se couchent,

Comme jours s'élèvent, les journées qui
Ne reviennent jamais—
Sauf dans le centre de Paris
Quand deviennent si gais

Le soleil de son rire en vol,
La lune de son éclat,
L'étoile de son sourire qui colle
La vie qui ni s'en va

Ni disparaît—car elle, en moi,
Jusqu'à la fin du corps,
Existera partout, parfois
En chaleureux rapports ...

Quant à la beauté de l'amour:
À nous la Belle Époque—
En rêves de rêveries qui courent
À la chanson du Coque.

Daydream
[fifteen]

Beginning now you warm, in dance,
The cockles of my soul
In buds somehow in thorn you lance
From once desire's pole.

'Twas cold in my Antarctic clime,
Until your womb above
Let sunshine win hypnotic rhyme
Amidst your blooming glove:

My hands, so quick on keys, they rise
For come what brew may stream
Through loveliness, to auburn eyes—
The ones, in whom they dream.

Holly Days
[sixteen]

My heart is springing up, for thou
Art roving jolly ways
That cling together—ever now
Our grove in Holly Days!

You fill my life with better things—
You give me Life itself:
Yes, without you its wetter wings
Are dew upon a shelf ...

An elf's awakening in me,
To laugh at days that bled—
For thou art Holly good, you see
You smile ... in my head!

How Deep the Ocean!
[seventeen]

How long I took, sweet heart of gold,
To still and season thyme,
That surely thou, whom love cajoled
Up into climes that hope patrol'd,
Mix'd lemonade with lime.

My heart, it wasn't thine to seize,
But thou would'st not incline
Hope's resignation unto lees
Left breathing in a glass, to freeze
Desire on the vine

Of deep in love true ocean's art
Necessity will buy
Inside so tremulous the heart
Of us—too just to ever part,
Lest we become a lie

For tangles in a cup of tea,
Free duty in the foal
Whose peace is ever, utterly,
Unable to unclutter thee
From artefact, or knoll.

Her Miracle
[eighteen]

I feel keen to be a man—
As mustard longs for bread:
Her miracle is where began
My heart to draw on her elan,
And suffer love instead.

When, suddenly, my chosen pump
To gold, from lead, she wrought—
Remembering my frozen stump
She made to swell, she made to thump,
In tidal waves of thought.

And so, if I, a man right now,
Am standing tall for Her—
'Tis but a Goddess words allow,
In veneration's hold, somehow,
Godiva to defer.

Queen
[nineteen]

I love a woman—call her Emma:
In my heart I see her there;
Inside my soul, a little tremor
Rocks the fox within his lair.

I broke her heart, one day gone by;
Just one day more, if it were mine,
I'd sip her chalice, willing die,
To taste her sorcery divine.

For I am now a King forgone,
A flounder in Fortuna's net,
Who spies a Mate, but takes a Pawn—
To miss his Queen, and kiss regret.

Enchantress
[twenty]

Emma's an enchantress, she
Is putting in a spell
My body's trick I can't rest, the
Rasputin in my dell.

In vagabondage to despair
I walk'd a crooked mile;
Now love is come to woo me where
I'm waiting on her smile.

She liveth love: To be her slave,
I will not err to make
The Hermitage—for what I crave
Is only hers to bake.

They say she is a dream come true—
To me she is a drug
For whom I hope my cream'll do
What sunshine's kiss'll hug.

Charlottchen
[twenty-one]

Wo bleibt, mein Gott, Charlottchen?
Es spritzt in meinem Kopf
Um Siegel für Klamottchen—
Die Tastatur am Zopf

Für Weisheit nie ohnmächtig,
Für Witz ein off'nes Buch
Hervorragend, so prächtig
Wie ein zu weites Tuch

Von Vornherein echt richtig,
Im Nachhinein schon wahr—
Was ich empfinde wichtig
Auf Parties, wo Hurra

Das Wort ist unter andern,

Was darauf mich erpicht,

Als beiden lässt umwandern

Ein Zwinkern im Gesicht!

Two Faces
[twenty-two]

Life eternal?
Gimme now!
It's dark outside—
You'll see
Her better fall
For Emmental,
Lest daylight
Comfort thee.

Miss Taylor's Lane
[twenty-three]

O Mr Churchill, pray for death
To neither as the end
Come wittingly—till stale breath
Aspire to ascend.

True love, above a cherry
To never be forgot:
They dig you, then they bury
What sunshine couldn't knot.

Be careful what you wish for—
Life's like that, don't you see?
A heart of gold's a dish for
The celibate in me!

And now, I cherish Emma:
Love's whispers mine to chart—
Daguerreotype's dilemma
Forever thine, sweet heart.

Emma James Robert
[twenty-four]

They couldn't write a word, for you
Put all their crits to shame:
The truth they spoke was never true,
Their cynicism lame—
Their ampersands & talismans
Pathetically tame.

You are the Lover of the Lambs,
The Keeper of the Flame,
The Loveliest of All the Rams,
And Number One in Name.

You studied hard, you chose to be
Much better than the blest—
Who, seeing only clothes that we
Remove beneath the canopy
Of starry eyes, in sanity,
Find one another best.

Love is but a fleeting glance
Of what so, now forever,
Doth lead my heart in ev'ry dance
We love, for life, together.

Emma, Queen of Heaven
[twenty-five]

Emma, Queen of Heaven, thou
Art lovelier than light
Uplifting my forever now
In orisons of white.

I think on thee, and joy is mine
To cradle in my soul;
Consider me: this boy is thine—
I have no other goal ...

On Earth we shall together live,
Till mortal days be done:
What sunshine their endeavour give
Is only just begun

For heart and soul of beauty such
Reposeth deep within
The one I love—a rose to touch,
And majesty to win!

Brand New Day
[twenty-six]

Another day—I hoped, in faith,
For you to ring my bell;
I turn'd it on, saw love escape
Not ever, to dispel

My hopelessness, my helplessness,
Together lost at sea
Betwixt the kelp and shellfishes
Ours only lent to free ...

So, Lover of My Cells, my God,
Oh, how I ache to—Gee!
Well, look into your eyes—why not?
For all eternity.

Courting Candles
[twenty-seven]

My Love, you were not what before
I knelt upon one knee
To make of love the concert raw—
In serendipity

To kiss your brow, to touch your cheek,
Lest transience of you,
O Sunshine, call the Florist weak
For knotting bunches too

Despotic, for the Man your prime
Inclusion might delight—
Erotic candles courting rhyme
For dark the sacred night.

Two Women
[twenty-eight]

Two women in the world there are,
Some say, yet I demur:
Oh, twinkle, twinkle little star
Forevermore in her—

The loveliness inside a pose
That urges to escape,
Reunifying sun and rose
In dew upon her nape ...

To sing a song, a while we
May wonder at her arts;
But where she speaks of rivalry,
One comes, and one departs.

Love in a Heart
[twenty-nine]

'Tis love in a heart which I cannot refute;

Let anyone tell me she doesn't there live:

Imaginings, clouds in the sky that pollute,

As light from a lantern no star will for-
give—

The moments of emptiness, Eros alone,

Surviving the shipwreck and drifting to
shore,

Yet reeling his heart in, to find but a
stone—

Lest sanity rescue what Psyche ignore,

I love thee unbearably, hopelessly, true:

Eternity beateth, a pris'ner within

The sunshine asparkle, to marry the dew

In whispering loveliness somewhat akin

To hillocks of hemlock on which I must dine—

Bewitching is hope, when the spell is divine!

Forgive Me, Lover
[thirty]

I said I'd never break it—
Your heart's the reason why
Nobody can mistake it:
Forgive me, Lover, I

Saw ghosts where only beauty
Knew loveliness within
The woman, in whom truly
Forgiveness dares to win!

Mere Ink
[thirty-one]

Mere ink aflow from mere my pen
Is ever bound to be
Regretful of its origin,
Bethought unworthily

Evoking thee in syllables
So silly, so uncouth—
Unequal to yon daffodils
That dance in gentle youth ...

Why part from truth? A lesser me
Doth beat for thee again;
Thy heart, lest ruth, ineffably,
Compete, requiteth then!

Lavender
[thirty-two]

In sleep no words retrieve her lips:
Concupiscence will heed
What deeply stirs, bequeathing hips
To honeysuckle mead—

Who wishes but to share the night
In dreams that never end,
To keep endeavour more polite
Than thoughts he cannot mend ...

Go thither, love her, lent of hours—
Loquacious sleeping form:
Both lavender the scent of flow'rs,
And linen, keeping warm.

Romance
[thirty-three]

I'll play you on the white keys:
Love dancing in the air
Shall infiltrate the night, seize
What chances to be there

Within your heart of pure gold—
As deep as any bed
Beneath the oceanic fold
To whom the sky be wed ...

Now, reverie's romance, in bud,
Through absence can but woo
Of mem'ry's flood the merry cud
I'm chewing on ... with you!

Honeysuckle Heart
[thirty-four]

If words be mine t'impart
Love beating in my soul,
A honeysuckle heart
In thee's to play a rôle:

A heart as honey sweet,
Thy person like as much—
How is the Paraclete
Himself to ponder such?

To take a dose of love's
To take a whiff of thee:
The holiest of doves
A rake's periphery!

Emma, No Dilemma
[thirty-five]

A heart of pure art;
A collage in my soul:
To stay, to never part
From thee—in whose patrol

Doth find a new beginning
One, teaching me to love
Sweet woman wondrous, winning
Desire for a glove

Restoring hope for sunshine—
'Tis rising on this day:
True eloquence begun, wine
To sip on—let us pray ...

"Emma"
[thirty-six]

The loveliest word,
The loveliest face;
Pls carry my sword—
Pls carry my mace:

I'll put you to music,
I'll rock you to sleep;
If ever you're too sick
To smile or weep

Let touch make you healthy,
If such you incline:
In poverty wealthy—
This all in me thine.

Gold
[thirty-seven]

What sunlight, on a rainy day,
Tonight doth clothe her eve:
She takes my hand, and I'm away
To what's on heaven's sleeve ...

She is a flower in the wet
That's pelting from above—
They say the sun can never set
To not yet prize a dove

To take into Eternity,
To love and to behold—
My Pilgrimage on Earth to see
A rainbow, through her gold.

She Says I am Her King
[thirty-eight]

I love a woman, she loves me,
She says I am her King—
Howbeit lemons, in my tea,
Are tracing honey's wing

Here in my heart, a lovely hope's
Rebounding back and forth
On Terra Firma's slipp'ry slopes
And onto Heaven's shores

Where thou, my Lady, knights debate
Through longest clovers toss'd,
In time to stop within innate
Serrated rivers cross'd—

And that for thee, the one for whom
Desire, hoarse in love,
Is wearing in devotion's bloom
For Him and Her above

Who ought to know that deep inside
The skybird's underway:
Too many lion cubs for pride
To mesmerize his prey.

Emma's Eyes
[thirty-nine]

What sunlight in my soul;
What sunshine in her dews:
What artistry's patrol
Her Majesty's "J'accuse!"

Methinks I see her rose
Beneath the snows that hide
True love on twinkle-toes—
So, come let her abide

Within my heart aflame,
So glittering a prize
I scarce can put name
To Emma's velvet eyes.

Love in Creation
[forty]

Love isn't blowing in the wind;
It doesn't rule the seas:
Your love is sweet as tamarind
Aflutter on the breeze:

Thee must our God have left till last
To lovingly create—
Let he or she be first to cast
The comely tree we ate

Into the Fire of Contempt:
To not be here at all
Would be for liars—none exempt—
A better way to fall.

Does She Know?
[forty-one]

Does she know how much I love her,
Far away in slumber deep?
If walls in Jericho must tumble,
Keep her safe, my God, in sleep!

I wish upon a star so lovely,
She was made for clothing it:
Bouquets of bushes, high above me,
Catch the rose proposing it ...

My cards I lay upon her table:
Father Time, too cool to kiss,
Will end my days preferring Abel—
However Cain may howl and hiss!

"Charlotte"
[forty-two]

Men with muscles, senses five,
Mostly come from moons on Mars;
Woman, Queen of Hill and Hive,
Fancies men with fancy cars ...

Yet I, abominable case—
Wanton, wooing some unknown—
Lost the sprint, but won the race's
Lamborghini, born to groan ...

Let God come first, to love or fear—
Depending on your wont, I guess:
Yet she will ever hold me dear,
In thinking of her loveliness.